Alfred's Basic Piano Library

Christmas Book · Level

P *i a n^o

Selected and Edited by E. L. Lancaster & Morton Manus

This book may be used by students in Level 3 of Alfred's Basic Piano Library or in the fourth book of any method.

The enduring charm of the Christmas season brings out the need for composers to express their feelings in newly-created Christmas music each year. Over the past century, many of these songs have become as well-known and loved as the traditional carols.

For this *Top Hits Christmas* series (Levels 1B, 2, 3, 4) we have selected only those new musical favorites that have become a permanent part of the Christmas season, and arranged them for young piano students. When combined with the traditional carols available in Alfred's *Merry Christmas!* Series (Levels 1B, 2, 3, 4), piano students have at their fingertips all the music they would want to perform during the holiday season.

PROGRESSIVE ORDER: When Christmas music can teach and reinforce the musical concepts students are studying, it is doubly beneficial. There is no need to play pieces above or below the appropriate grade level, or to take a break from proper piano study, to enjoy playing Christmas music.

With this in mind, this book has been written to fit precisely with the music fundamentals as they are introduced in Level 3 of Alfred's Basic Piano Library. Although the songs are placed in approximate order of difficulty, they may be played in any order.

The arrangers and editors wish the teacher, student and parents a very merry Christmas and hope you will enjoy the new and special arrangements of Christmas music found in this book.

Published by
HAL•LEONARD®
CORPORATION

Distributed by

Alfred Publishing Co., Inc.

ISBN 0-7390-0402-6

Silver Bells

from the Paramount Picture THE LEMON DROP KID

Words and Music by
Jay Livingston and Ray Evans
Arr. by Sharon Aaronson

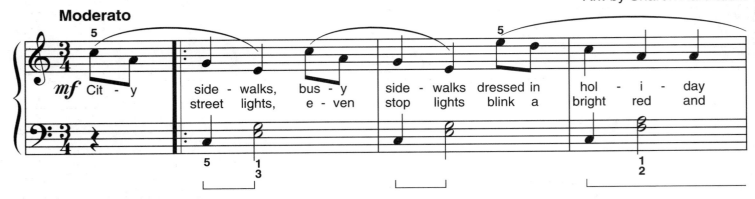

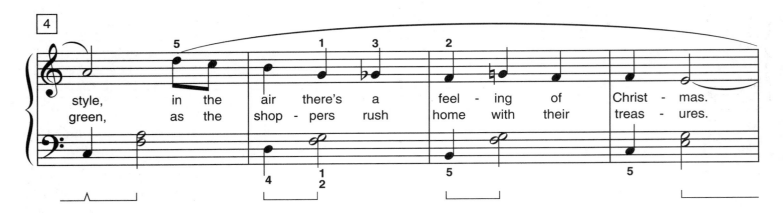

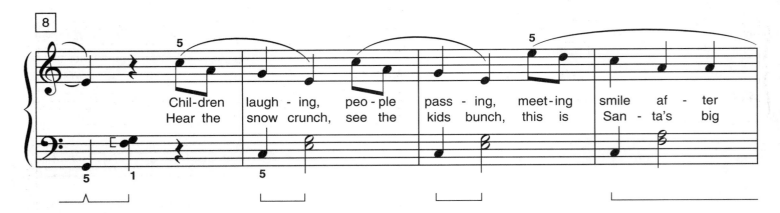

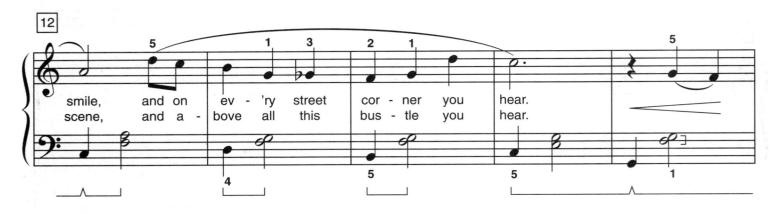

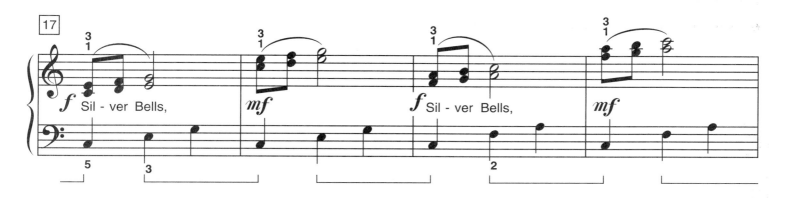

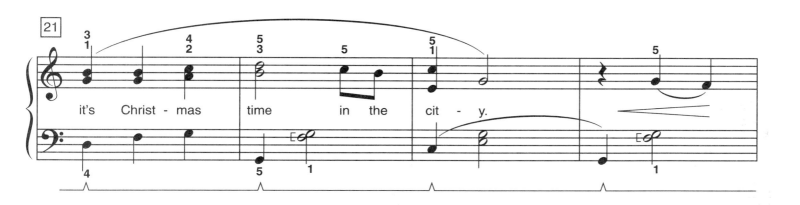

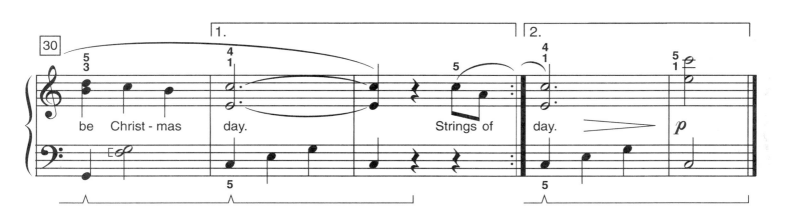

Frosty the Snow Man

Words and Music by
Steve Nelson and Jack Rollins
Arr. by Dennis Alexander

5

Rudolph the Red-Nosed Reindeer

Music and Lyrics by Johnny Marks
Arr. by Tom Gerou

A Holly Jolly Christmas

Music and Lyrics by Johnny Marks
Arr. by Martha Mier

Jingle-Bell Rock

Words and Music by
Joe Beal and Jim Boothe
Arr. by George Peter Tingley

*Optional: Play eighth notes a bit unevenly, in a "lilting" style: long short long short, *etc.*

I'll Be Home for Christmas

Words and Music by
Kim Gannon and Walter Kent
Arr. by Martha Mier

I Saw Mommy Kissing Santa Claus

Words and Music by Tommie Connor
Arr. by George Peter Tingley

Shake Me I Rattle
(Squeeze Me I Cry)

Words and Music by
Hal Hackady and Charles Naylor
Arr. by Sharon Aaronson

Moderately slow

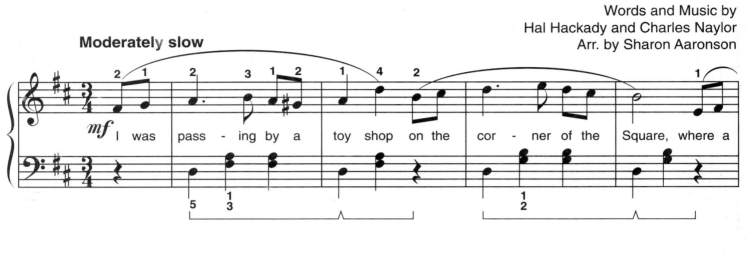

mf I was pass - ing by a toy shop on the cor - ner of the Square, where a

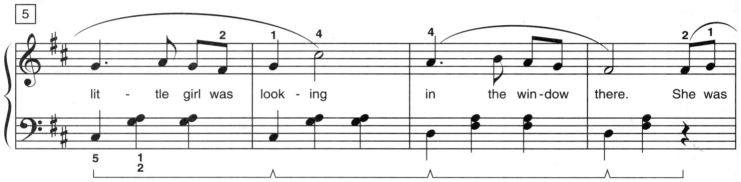

lit - tle girl was look - ing in the win - dow there. She was

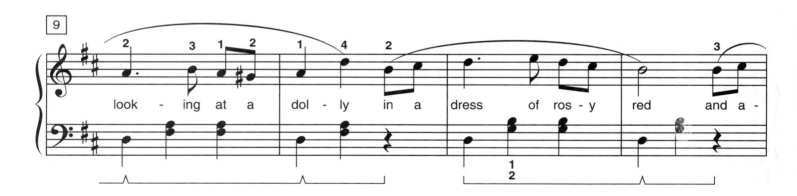

look - ing at a dol - ly in a dress of ros - y red and a -

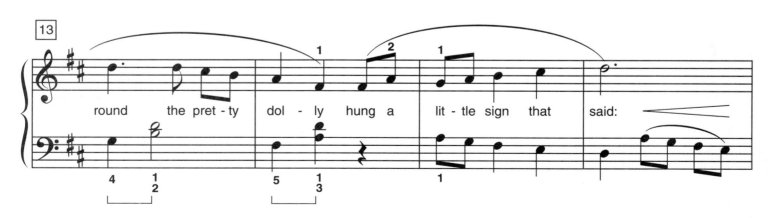

round the pret - ty dol - ly hung a lit - tle sign that said:

2. I recalled another toy shop on a square so long ago
   Where I saw a little dolly that I wanted so.
   I remembered, I remembered how I longed to make it mine
   And around that other dolly hung another little sign:
   SHAKE ME, I RATTLE, SQUEEZE ME, I CRY.
   I had counted my pennies, just a penny shy.
   SHAKE ME, I RATTLE, SQUEEZE ME, I CRY.
   Please take me home and love me!

3. It was late and snow was falling as the shoppers hurried by
   Past the girlie at the window with her little head held high.
   They were closing up the toy shop as I hurried thru the door
   Just in time to buy the dolly that her heart was longing for!
   SHAKE ME, I RATTLE, SQUEEZE ME, I CRY.
   And I gave her the dolly that we both had longed to buy.
   SHAKE ME, I RATTLE, SQUEEZE ME, I CRY.
   Please take me home and love me!

Do You Hear What I Hear

Words and Music by
Noel Regney and Gloria Shayne
Arr. by Tom Gerou

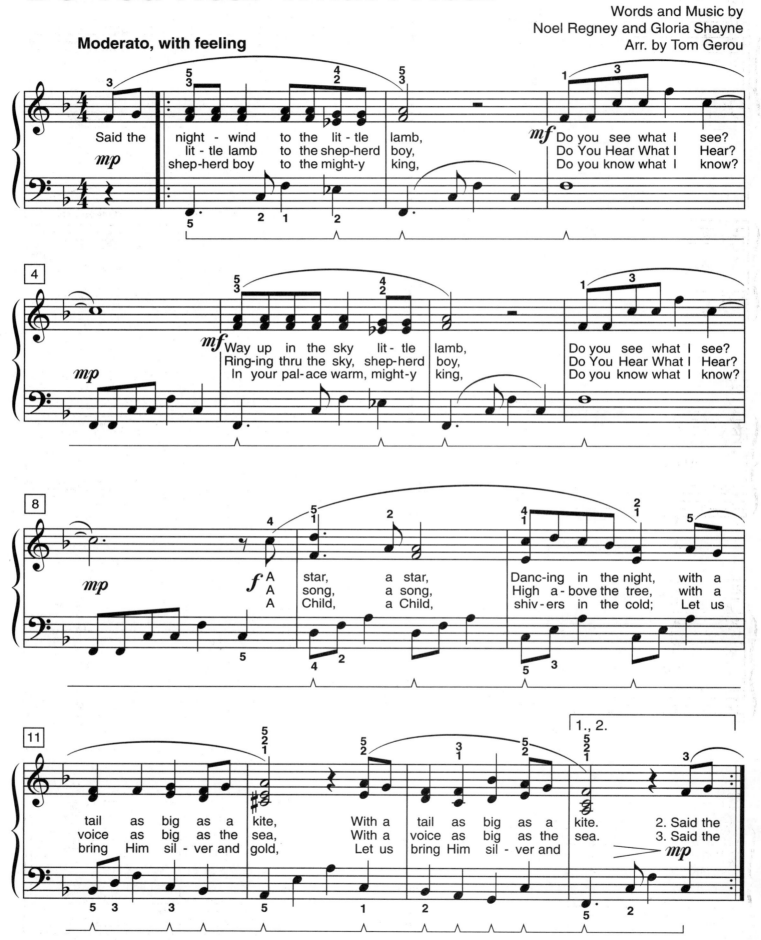

Caroling, Caroling

Words by Wihla Hutson
Music by Alfred Burt
Arr. by Tom Gerou

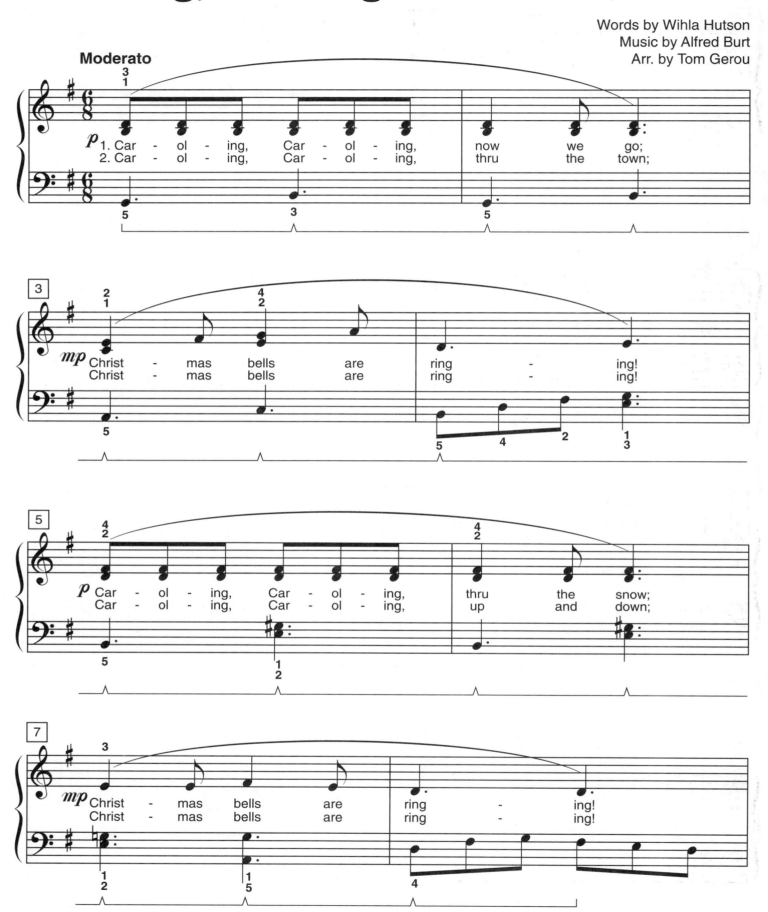

Parade of the Wooden Soldiers

English Lyrics by Ballard MacDonald
Music by Leon Jessel
Arr. by Martha Mier

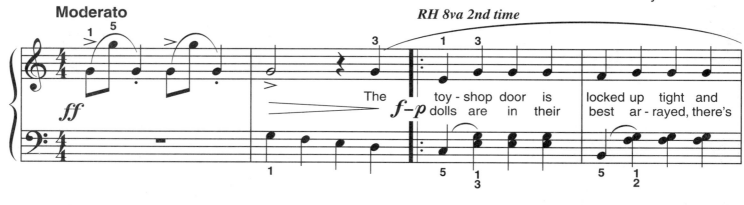

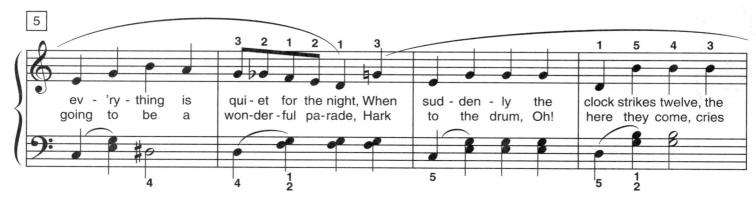

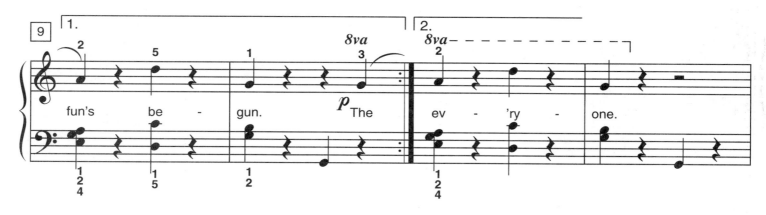

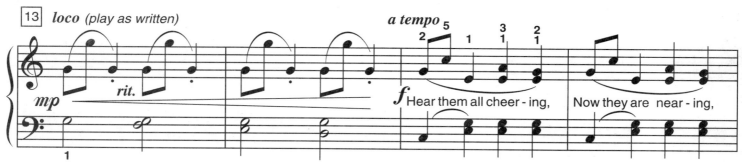

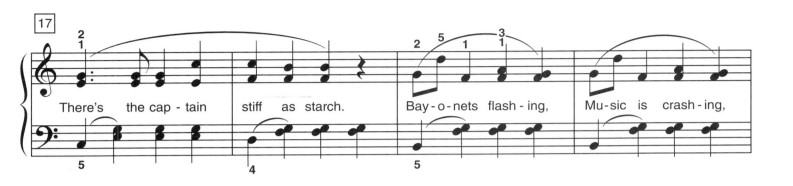

There's the cap - tain stiff as starch. Bay-o-nets flash-ing, Mu-sic is crash-ing,

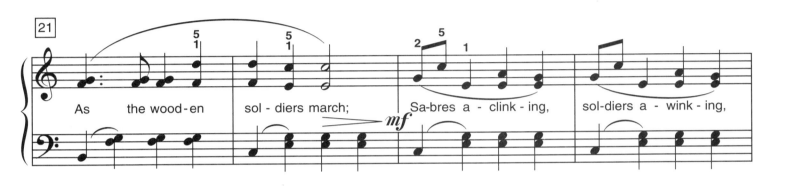

As the wood-en sol - diers march; Sa-bres a - clink-ing, sol-diers a - wink-ing,

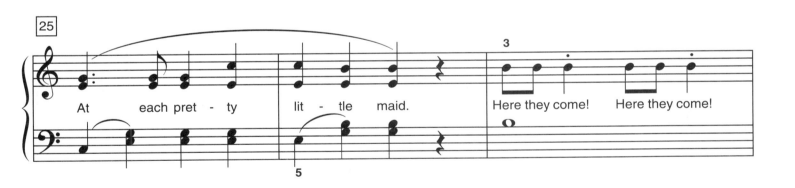

At each pret - ty lit - tle maid. Here they come! Here they come!

Here they come! Here they come! Wood - en sol-diers on pa - rade.

24

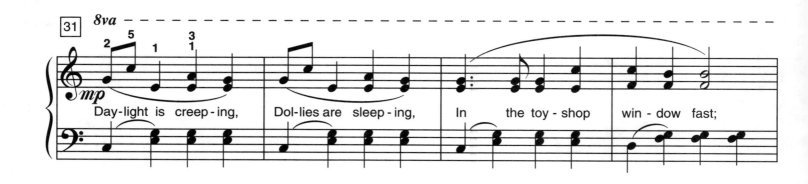

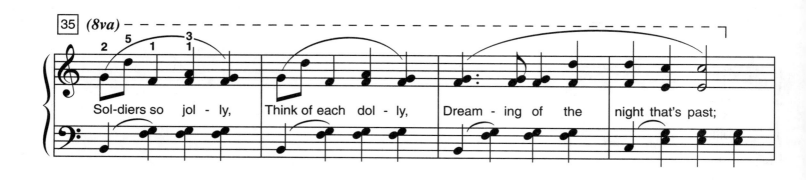

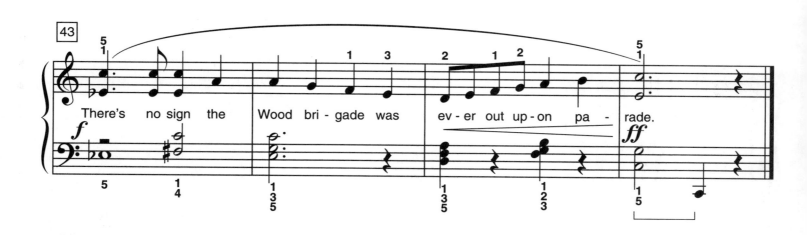